5	**ALL OF THE STARS**	Ed Sheeran
10	**SIMPLE AS THIS**	Jake Bugg
17	**LET ME IN**	Grouplove
27	**TEE SHIRT**	Birdy
30	**ALL I WANT**	Kodaline
42	**LONG WAY DOWN**	Tom Odell
46	**BOOM CLAP**	Charli XCX
51	**WHILE I'M ALIVE**	Strfkr
58	**OBLIVION**	Indians
64	**STRANGE THINGS WILL HAPPEN**	The Radio Dept.
71	**BOMFALLERALLA**	Afasi & Filthy
76	**WITHOUT WORDS**	Ray LaMontagne
82	**NOT ABOUT ANGELS**	Birdy
88	**NO ONE EVER LOVED**	Lykke Li
95	**WAIT**	M83
99	**BEST SHOT**	Birdy & Jaymes Young

ALL OF THE STARS

Words and Music by ED SHEERAN
and JOHN McDAID

* Recorded a half step lower

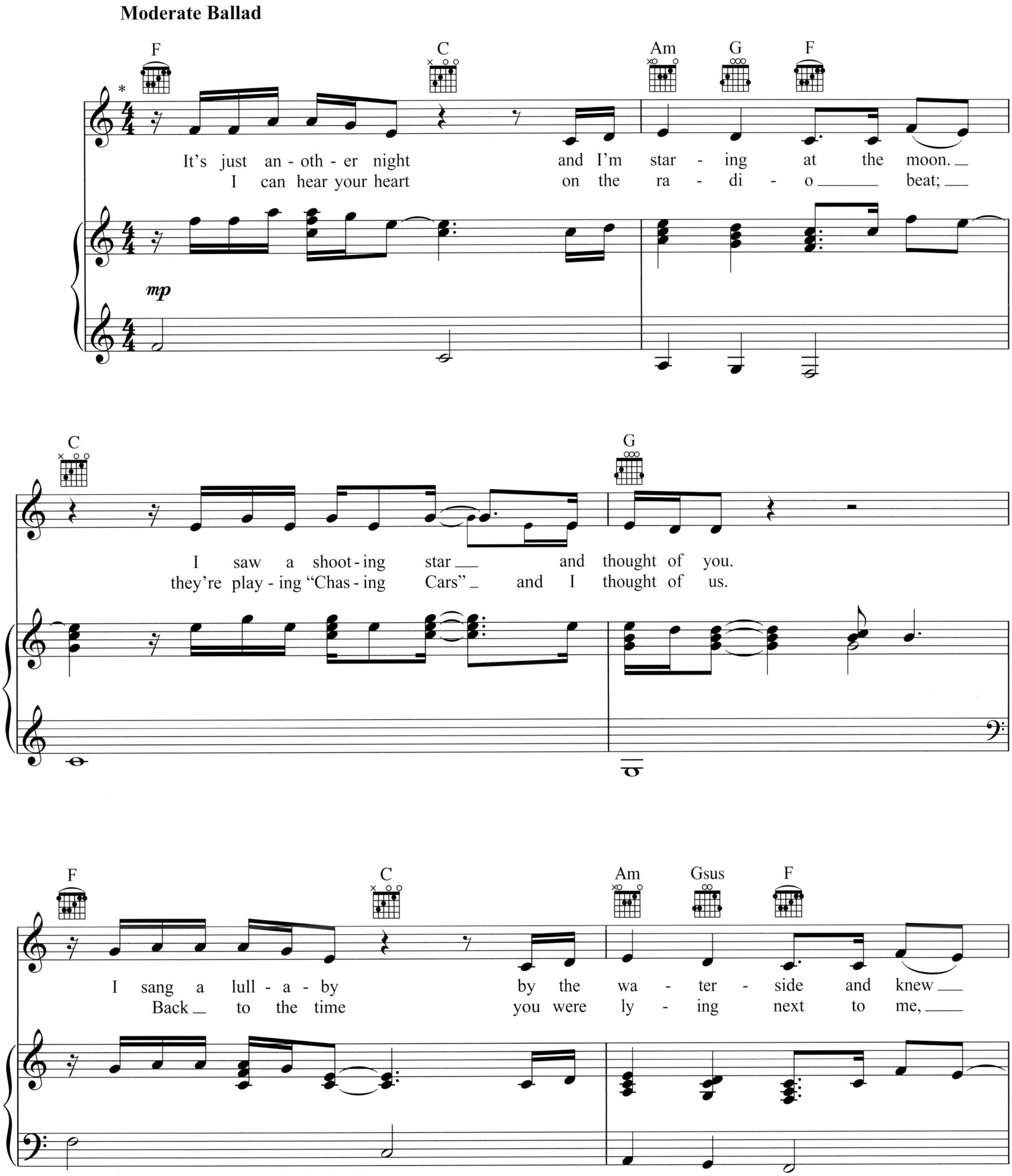

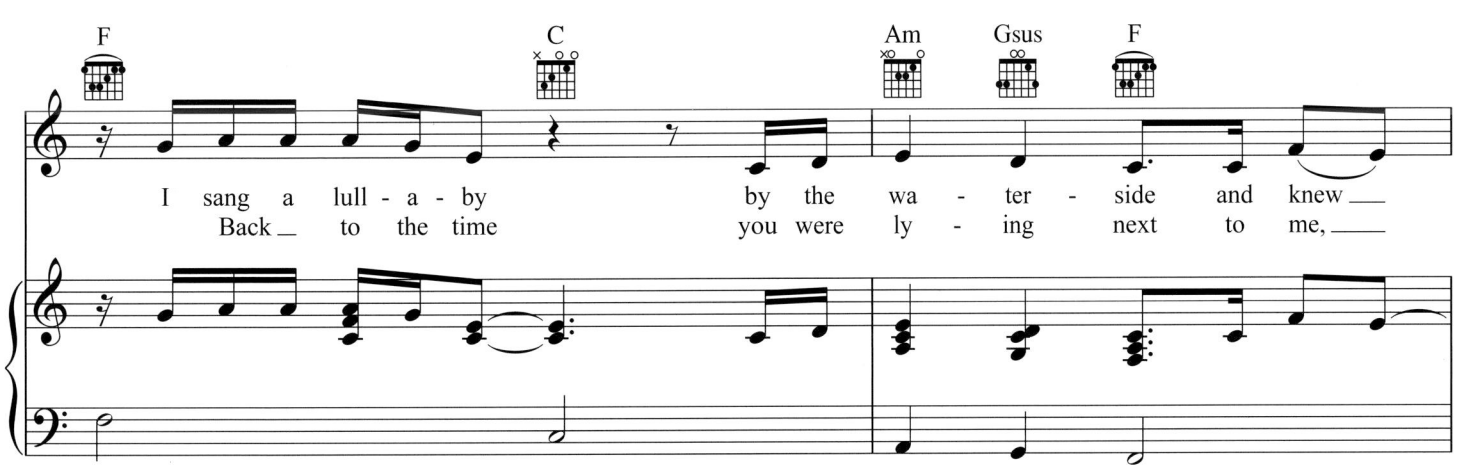

SIMPLE AS THIS

Words and Music by JAKE KENNEDY
and MATTHEW PRIME

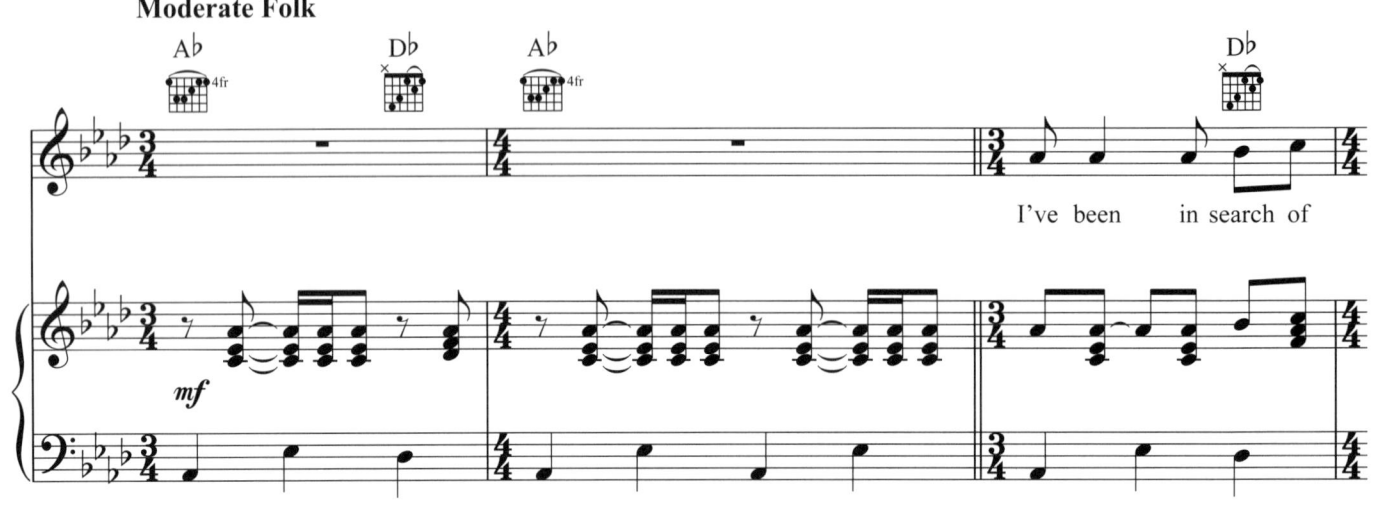

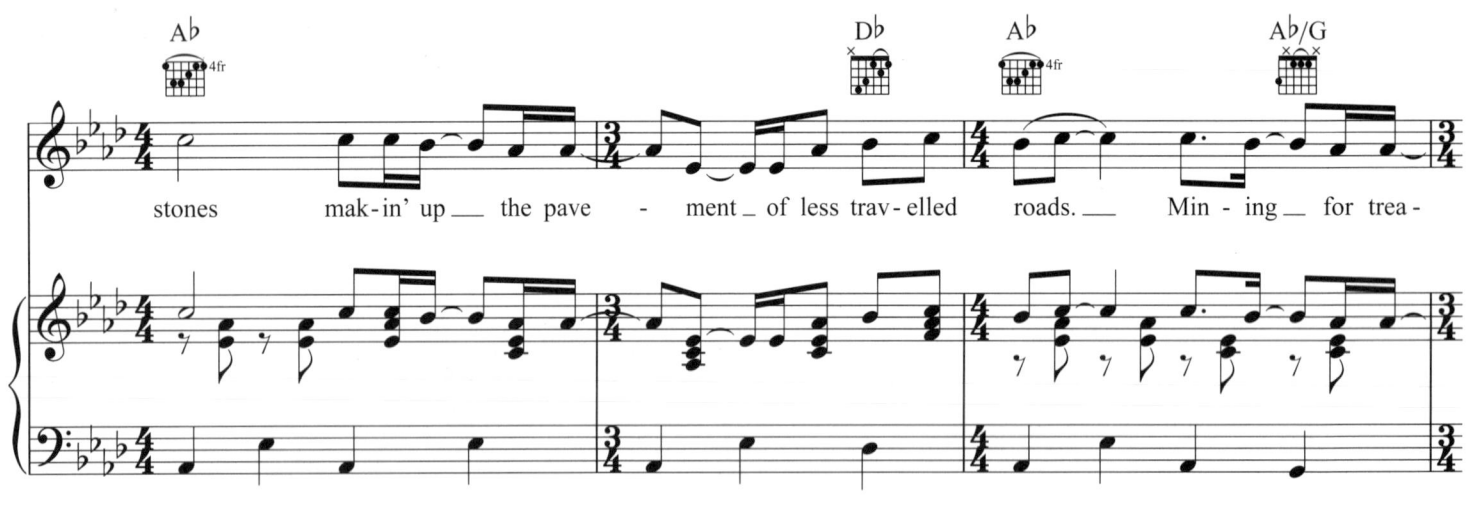

Copyright © 2014 Soul Kitchen Music Ltd. and Sony/ATV Music Publishing Limited UK
All Rights for Soul Kitchen Music Ltd. Administered Worldwide by Songs Of Kobalt Music Publishing
All Rights for Sony/ATV Music Publishing Limited UK Administered by Sony/ATV Music Publishing LLC, 424 Church Street, Suite 1200, Nashville, TN 37219
All Rights Reserved   Used by Permission

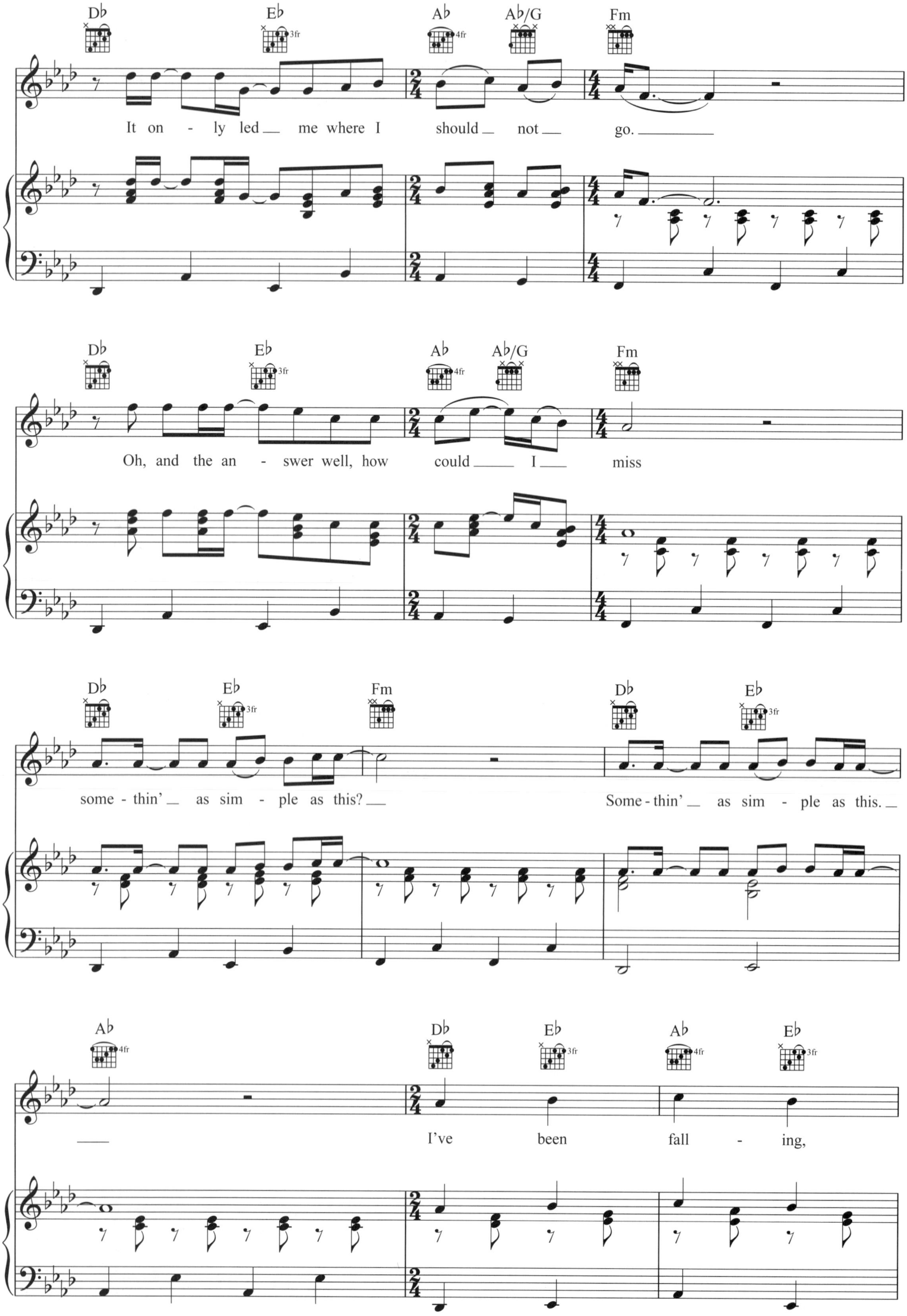
Db Eb Ab Ab/G Fm
3fr 4fr
It on - ly led me where I should not go.
Db Eb Ab Ab/G Fm
3fr 4fr
Oh, and the an - swer well, how could I miss
Db Eb Fm Db Eb
3fr 3fr
some - thin' as sim - ple as this?
Some - thin' as sim - ple as this.
Ab Db Eb Ab Eb
4fr 3fr 4fr 3fr
I've been fall - ing,

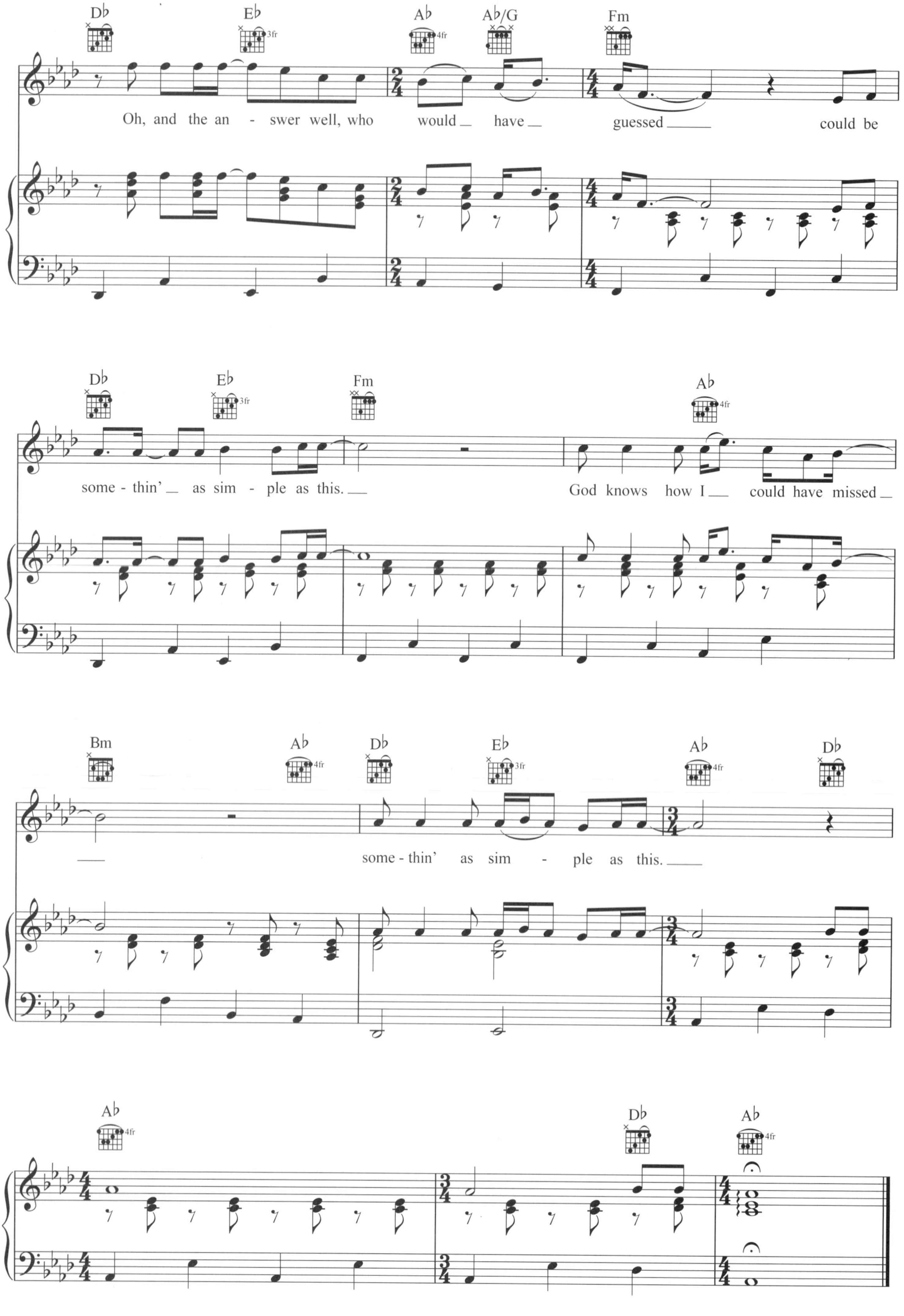
D♭ E♭ A♭ A♭/G Fm
3fr 4fr
Oh, and the an - swer well, who would have guessed could be
D♭ E♭ Fm A♭
3fr 4fr
some - thin' as sim - ple as this.
God knows how I could have missed
Bm A♭ D♭ E♭ A♭ D♭
4fr 3fr 4fr
some - thin' as sim - ple as this.
A♭ D♭ A♭
4fr 4fr

LET ME IN

Words and Music by CHRISTIAN ZUCCONI,
HANNAH HOOPER, RYAN RABIN,
ANDREW WESSEN and DANIEL GLEASON

* Recorded a half step lower

© 2014 WB MUSIC CORP., CHRISTIAN ZUCCONI PUBLISHING, MADAM H, NKOSI SIKELELI AFRIKA MUSIC,
ANDREW WESSEN PUBLISHING, DAN GLEASON PUB DESIGNEE and T C F MUSIC PUBLISHING, INC.
All Rights for CHRISTIAN ZUCCONI PUBLISHING, MADAM H, NKOSI SIKELELI AFRIKA MUSIC,
ANDREW WESSEN PUBLISHING and DAN GLEASON PUB DESIGNEE Administered by WB MUSIC CORP.
All Rights Reserved   Used by Permission

TEE SHIRT

Words and Music by JASMINE VAN DEN BOGAERDE
and DAN WILSON

Easy Ballad

In the morn-ing when you wake up, I
When I saw you, ev-'ry-one knew I

like to be-lieve you are think-ing of me.
liked the af-fect that you had on my eyes.

And when the sun comes through your win-dow, I
But no one else heard the way of your words or

© 2014 Good Soldier Songs Limited, Sugar Lake Music and T C F Music Publishing, Inc.
All Rights for Good Soldier Songs Limited in the U.S. and Canada Administered by WB Music Corp.
All Rights Reserved   Used by Permission

ALL I WANT

Words and Music by JAMES FLANNIGAN,
STEPHEN GARRIGAN, MARK PRENDERGAST
and VINCENT MAY

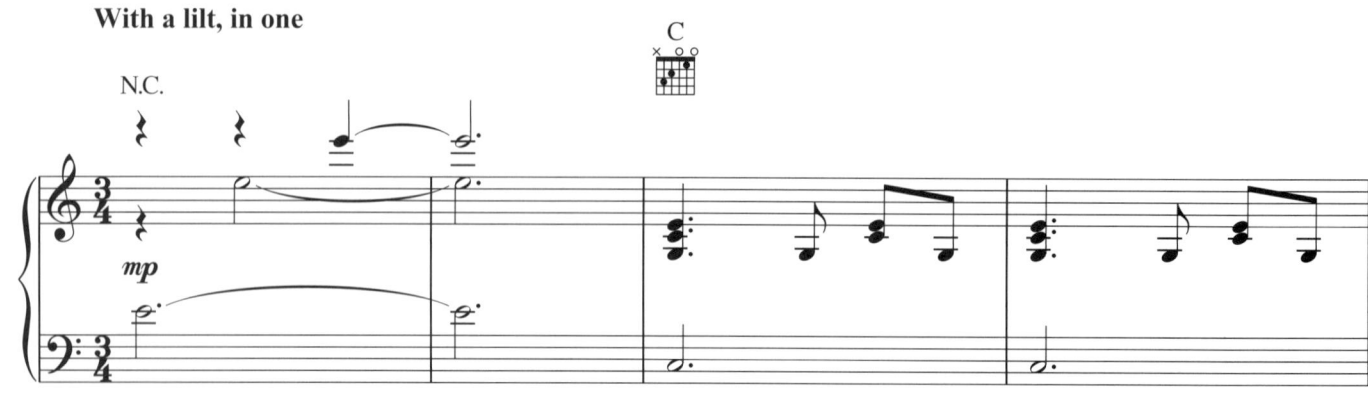

Copyright © 2012 B-Unique Music Ltd.
All Rights Administered Worldwide by Kobalt Songs Music Publishing and Songs Of Kobalt Music Publishing
All Rights Reserved   Used by Permission

Oh.

Oh.

Oh.

Oh.

Oh.

Oh.

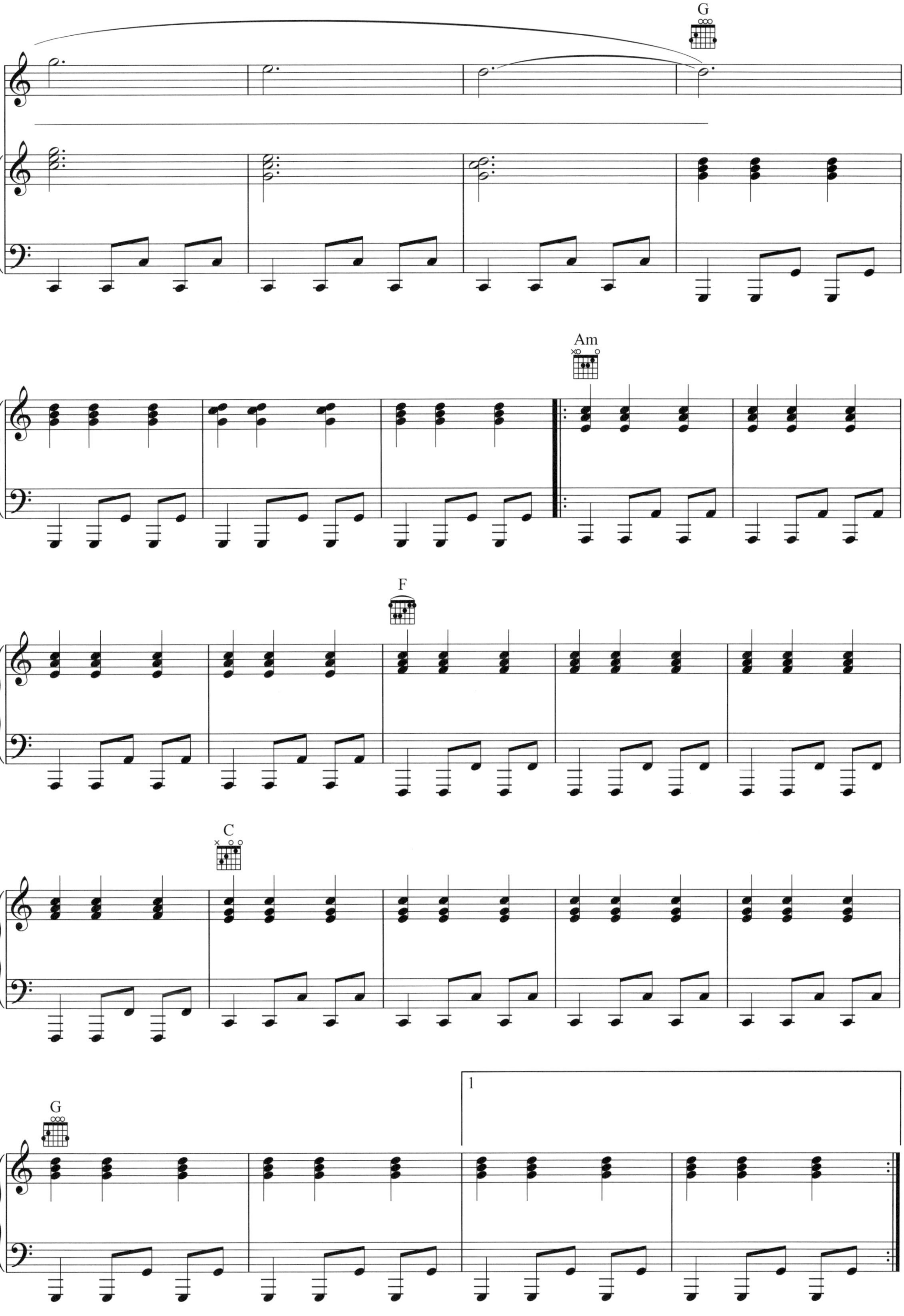
G
Am
F
C
G
1

But if you loved me, why'd you leave me? Take my bod-y, take my bod-y All I want is and all I _____ need is to find _____ some-bod-y, I'll find _____ some-bod-y like _____ you. _____

LONG WAY DOWN

Words and Music by
TOM ODELL

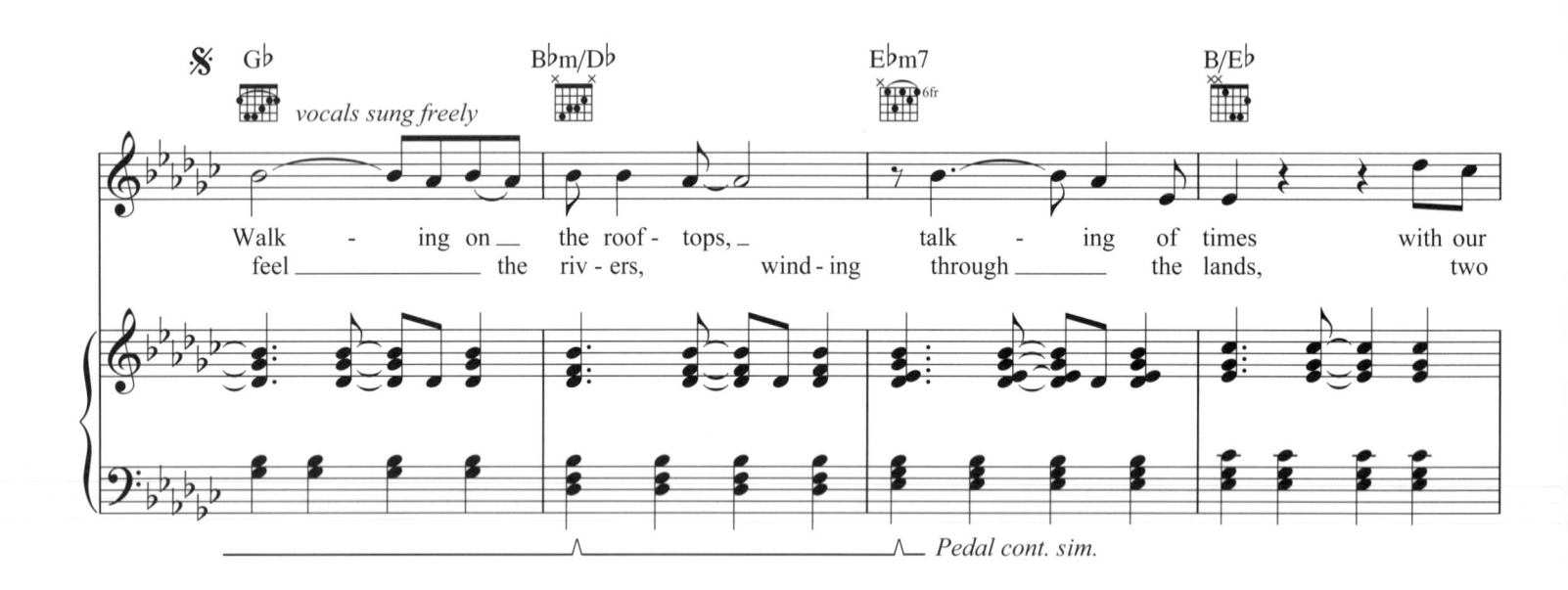

Moderately ♩=132

Walk-ing on the roof-tops, talk-ing of times with our
feel the riv-ers, wind-ing through the lands, two

eyes a glow-ing, like the cit-y lights, she
lines and a po-et, like a kind old rye, you know we could

© 2013 TOM ODELL MUSIC LTD.
All Rights in the U.S. and Canada Administered by WB MUSIC CORP.
All Rights Reserved   Used by Permission

stands ____ on the ledge, ____ she says, "it looks ____ so high," ____
talk ____ in that ____ lan-guage on-ly we un-der-stand, ____

you know ____ it's a... ____
you know ____ hon-ey ____ it's a... ____

Long way ____ down, ____ feels like a

long way ____ down, ____ it feels like a

G♭
G♭maj7
B/G♭
long way ________ down, yeah, _ like a
G♭
E♭m7
6fr
long way ________ down, ___ so hon - ey,
p
B♭m/D♭
B
D.S. al Coda
don't leave, _ don't ___ leave, please _ don't _ leave me now. _ Cuz I can
mp
p
CODA
G♭
G♭maj7
B
long way ________ down, you know that it's a
mp

G♭
E♭m
B♭m7/F
long way down, it feels like a
mf
G♭
G♭maj7
B
long way down oh, it feels like a
f
G♭
E♭m7
6fr
long way down so hon-ey,
mf
B♭m/D♭
B
don't leave, don't leave, please don't leave me now.
pp

BOOM CLAP

Words and Music by CHARLOTTE AITCHISON,
PATRIK BERGER, FREDRIK BERGER
and STEFAN GRASLUND

Moderate Pop Rock

Boom, boom, boom, clap.

You're picture-perfect blue, sun-bathing on the moon.
No silver or no gold could dress me up so good.
Stars shining as your bones il-lu-mi-
You're the glit-ter in the dark-ness of my

Copyright © 2014 Sony/ATV Sounds LLC, Indiscipline AB, Publishing Company TEN AB and Stefan Graslund Publishing Designee
All Rights on behalf of Sony/ATV Sounds LLC Administered by Sony/ATV Music Publishing LLC, 424 Church Street, Suite 1200, Nashville, TN 37219
All Rights on behalf of Indiscipline AB and Publishing Company TEN AB Administered by Kobalt Songs Music Publishing
International Copyright Secured   All Rights Reserved

E5
C♯m7
4fr
Asus2
Bsus
nate.
world.
First kiss just like a drug,
Just tell me what to do,
un - der your in - flu - ence.
I'll fall right in - to you.
You take me o - ver, you're the mag - ic in my
Go - ing un - der, cast a spell, just say the
N.C.
veins. This must be love.
word. I feel your love.
Boom clap, the sound of my heart. The
E
beat goes on and on and on and on. And boom clap, you make me feel good. Come on

E
C♯m7
4fr
Asus2
Bsus
to me, come on to me now. Boom clap, the sound of my heart. The
E
C♯m7
4fr
Asus2
Bsus
beat goes on and on and on and on. And boom clap, you make me feel good. Come on
1
E
Asus2
Bsus
to me, come on to me now.
E5
C♯m7
4fr
2
E
to me, come on to me now.

Lyrics:

You are the light, and I will fol-low.

You let me lose my shad-ow.

You are the sun, the glow-ing ha-lo.

And you keep burn-ing me up with all your love. Uh.

Boom clap, the sound of my heart. The beat goes on and on and on and on. And boom clap, you make me feel good. Come on to me, come on to me now.

Boom clap, the sound of my heart. The beat goes on and on and on and on. And boom clap, you make me feel good. Come on to me, come on to me now.

WHILE I'M ALIVE

Words and Music by KEIL CORCORAN,
JOSHUA HODGES, PATRICK MORRIS
and SHAWN GLASSFORD

Moderate Disco groove

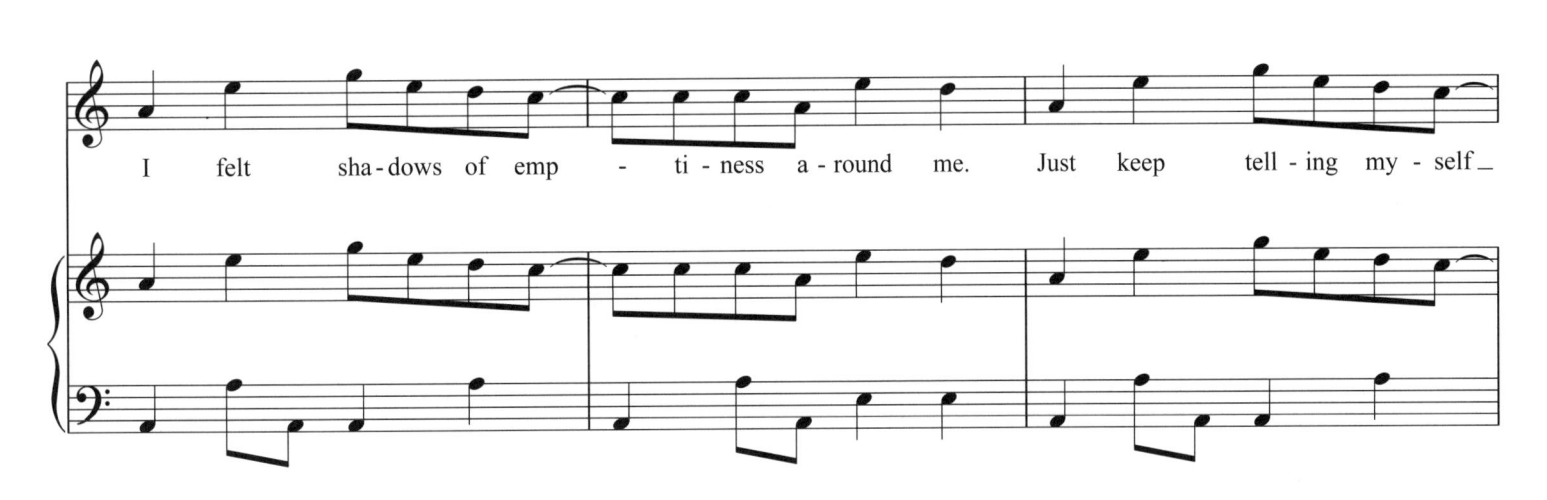

Ahh. Ahh.

Last night, all black and white when I was sleep-ing.

I felt sha-dows of emp-ti-ness a-round me. Just keep tell-ing my-self

Copyright © 2013 BMG Gold Songs, Kromdar Publishing, Strfkr, BMG Platinum Songs, Mr. Soeda and Tinchevy Music
All Rights Administered by BMG Rights Management (US) LLC
All Rights Reserved   Used by Permission

___ to live my life a-live. Like ev-'ry-thing else, ___ just keep on breath-ing and live. ___

Oh, ___ oh, ___ oh, ___

While I'm a-live, ___

I've got, I live my life. ___ While I'm a-live, ___

F Em Dm F Em Dm
the colors and the sound. While I'm a - live,
F Em Dm F Em Dm
To Coda
F Em Dm
I've got, I live my life. While I'm a - live, da, da, da, da.
N.C.
Ahh, ahh.
Am
Saw the way I would die while I was dream - ing.

Cold but hear-ing the sound that a heart beats. Keep on tell-ing my-self to live my life a-live. Like ev-'ry-thing else, just keep on breath-ing and live.

D.S. al Coda

CODA

da, da, da, da, da.

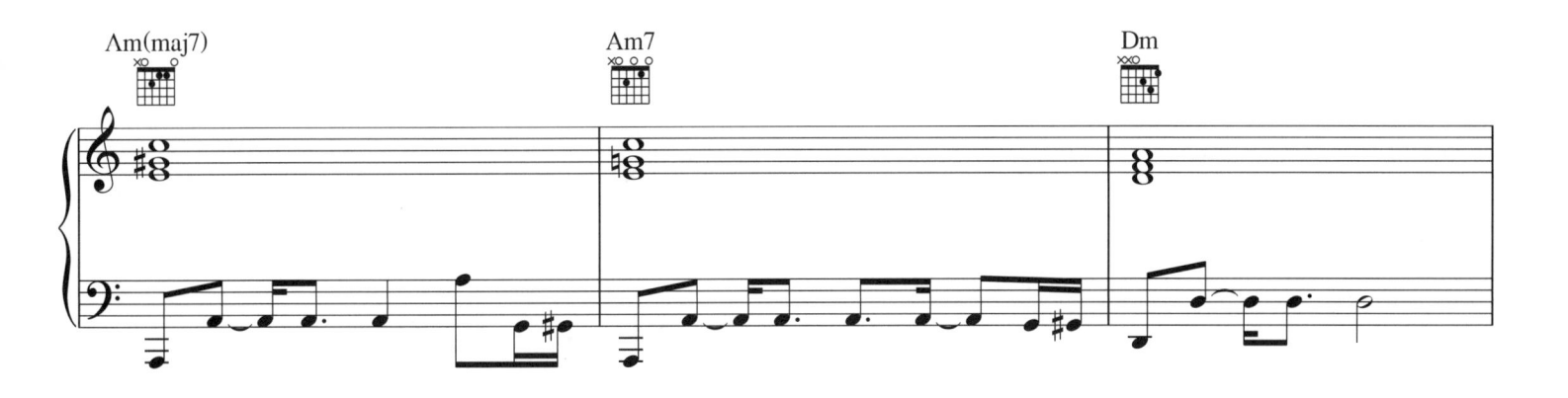

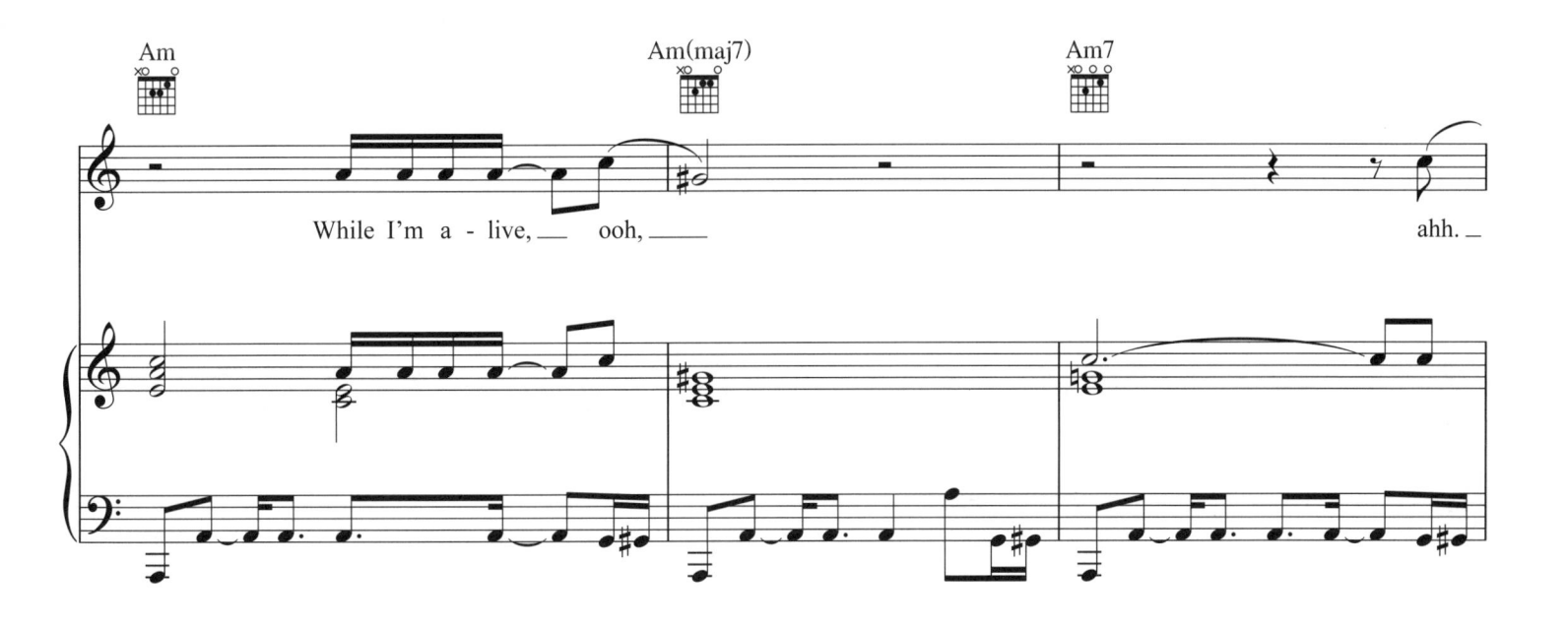

While I'm a - live, ___ ooh, ___ ahh. ___

Dm
Am
Am(maj7)
Am7
Dm
Am
While I'm a - live.
Am(maj7)
Am7
Dm
While I'm a - live.
Am
Am(maj7)
Am7
While I'm a - live.
While I'm a - live.

57

OBLIVION

Words and Music by
SOREN LOEKKE JUUL

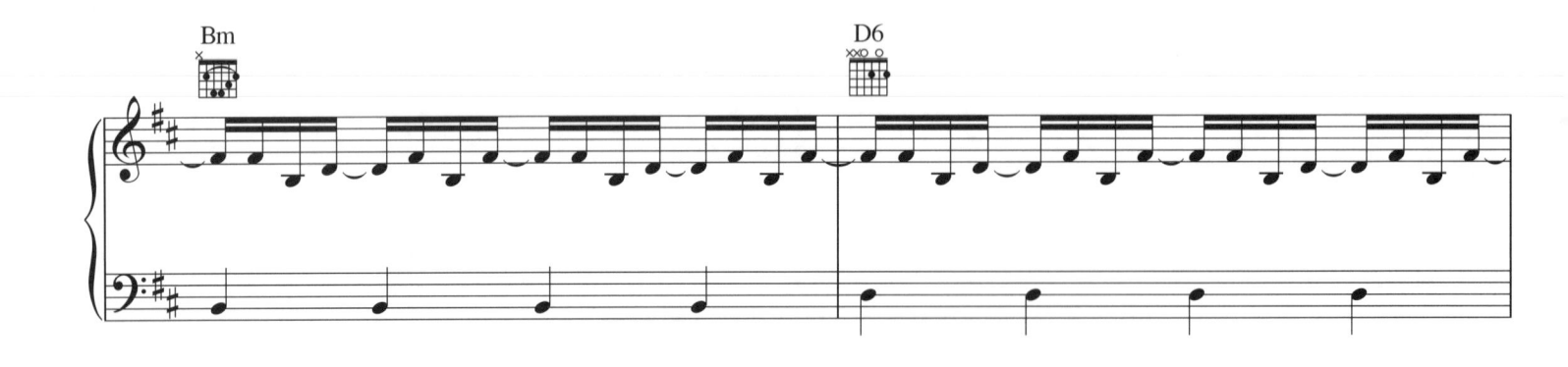

D
I be - lieve when I see some - thin', it can
Gmaj7
grow 'cause I see it in your eyes.
Bm
It be - longs.
D6
Speak, just to me 'cause we're
Gmaj9
now sprin - kled in the stars.

60

D

I can see _____ e-ven from a dis-tance. ___ It makes ___

Gmaj7

___ sense, ___ want you to ___ be mine. ___

Bm   **D6**

This will end. ___ Come, come clos-er. Let it

Gmaj9

go, let it feel ___ the wind. ___

Close to you, I'm home free, but it won't last. The future to be-long to one of us.

Start-ed out as noth-ing, soon to be the beau-ty of all stars.

62

Start-ed out as noth-ing, soon to be the beau-ty of all stars.

I'm in love with you I said in-to the void. I know you'll hear me soon and it will hear no more.

CODA

Start-ed out as noth-ing, _____ soon to be the beau-ty of all _____ stars. _____

Start-ed out as noth-ing, _____ soon to be the beau-ty of all _____ stars. _____

Repeat and Fade | **Optional Ending**

STRANGE THINGS WILL HAPPEN

Words and Music by
JOHAN DUNCANSON

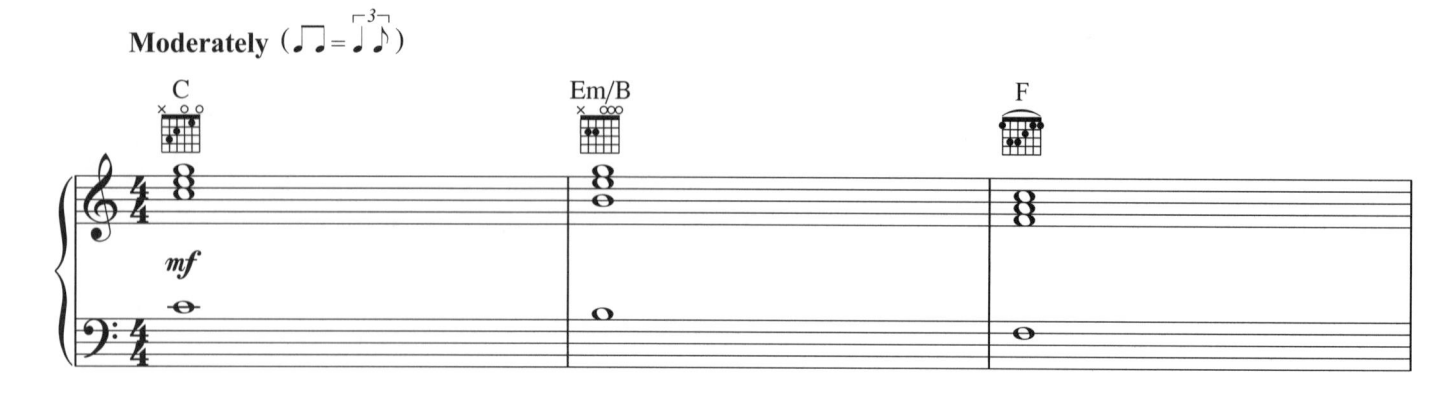

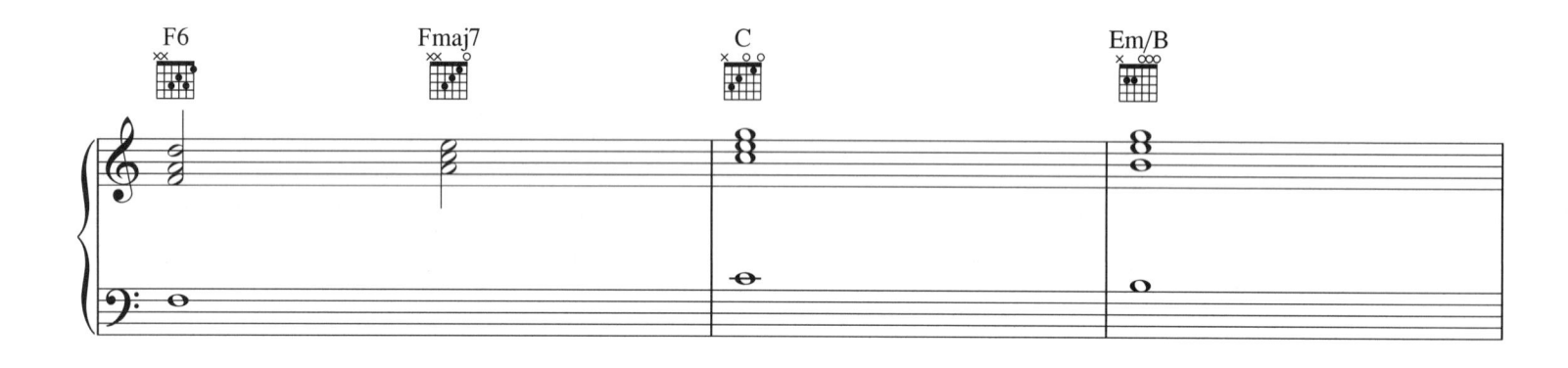

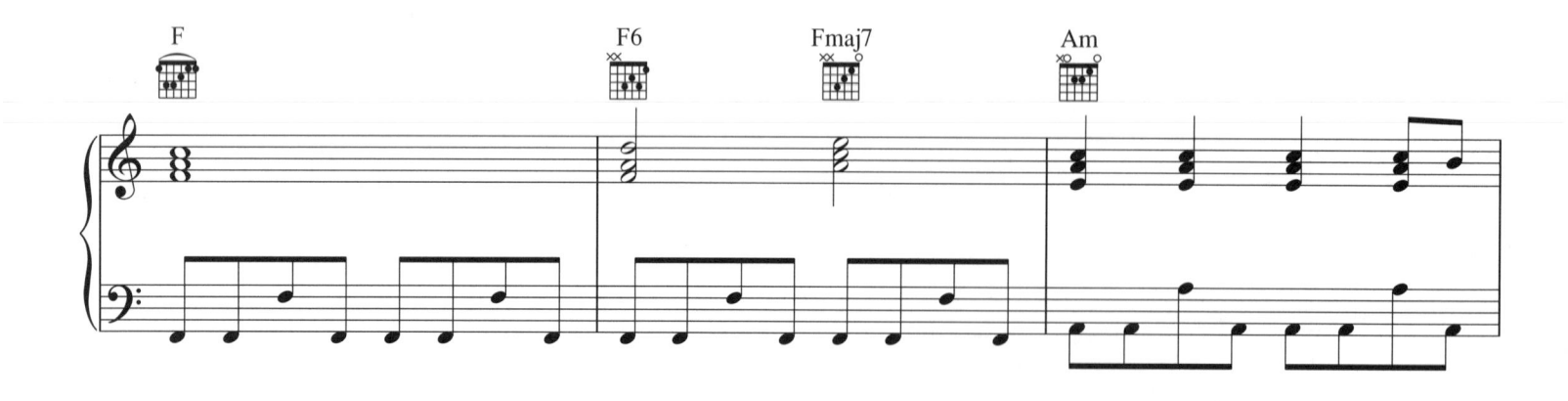

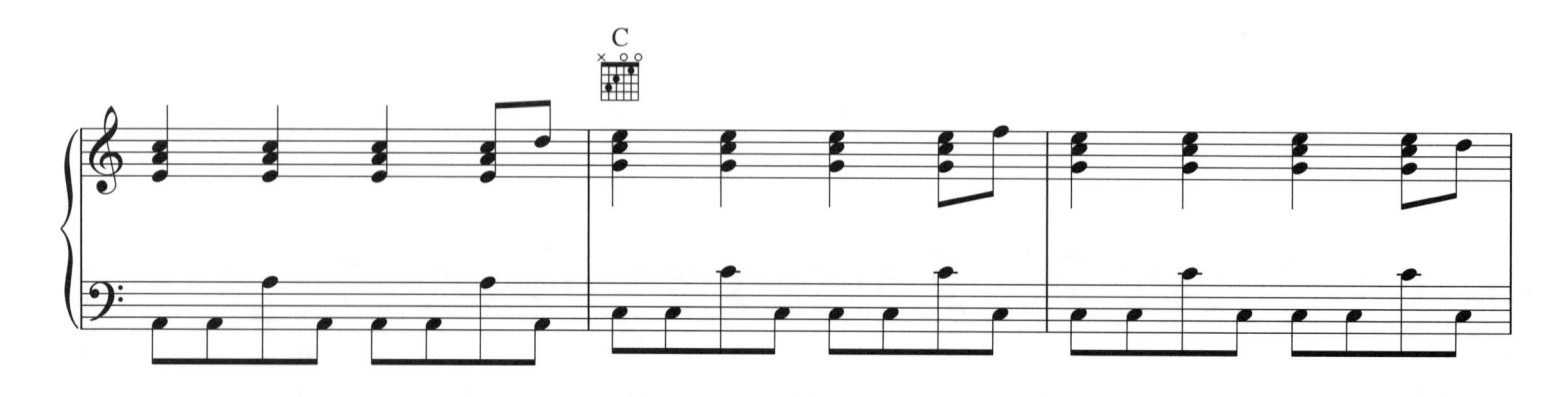

To -

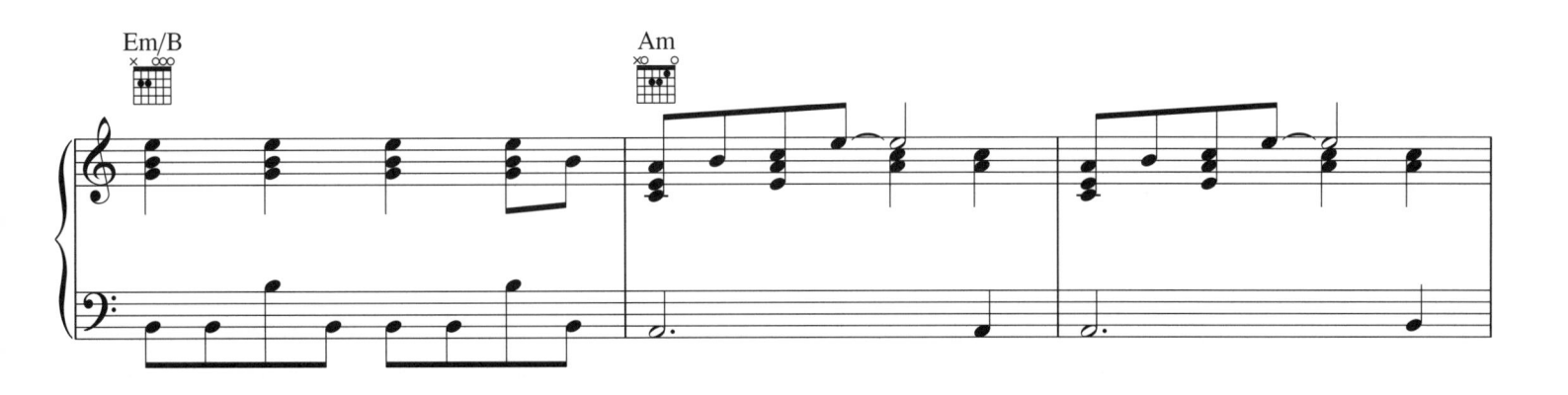

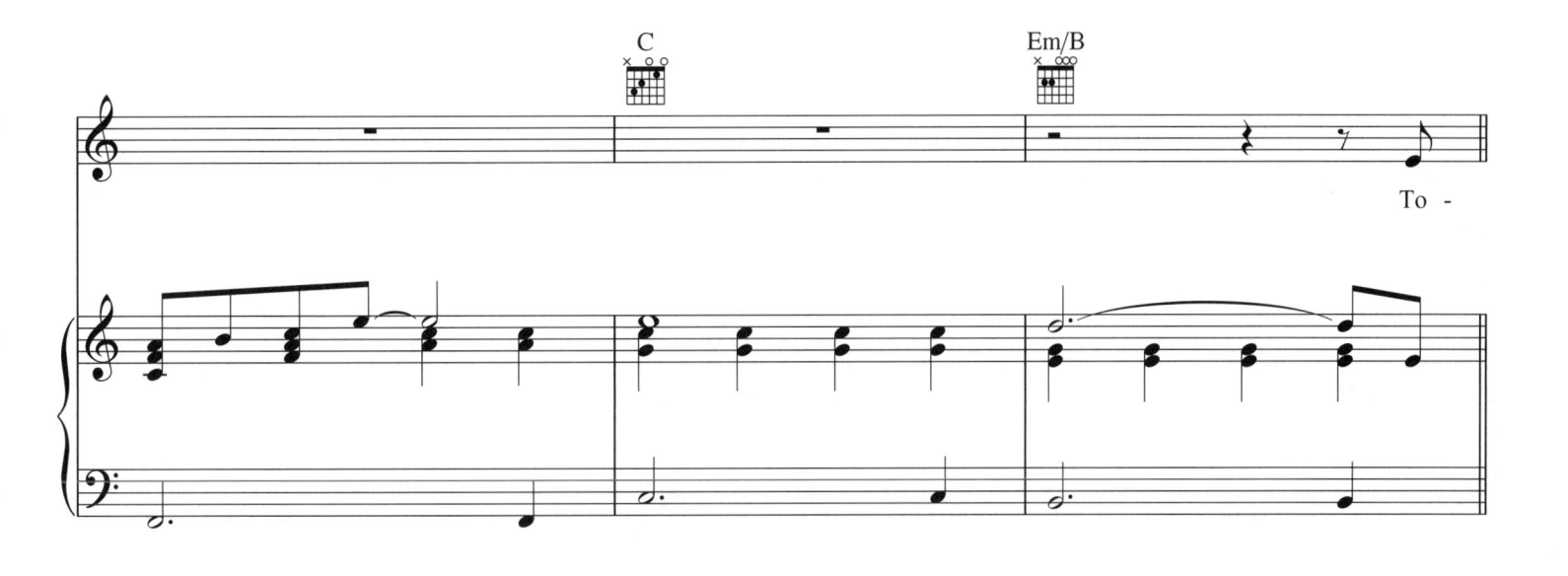

day was a pretty day.
day was a pretty day.

No dis-ap-point-ments, no ex-pec-ta-tions on your where-a-bouts. And oh,
Au-tumn comes with these slight sur-pris-es where your life might twist and turn.

did I let you go? Did it fi-nal-ly show
Hope to un-learn. Strange things will hap-

that strange things will hap-pen if
-pen if you let them come a-round

you let them. To-
and stick a-round.

day I didn't ev-en try to hide.

I'll stay here and nev-er push things to the side.

You can't reach me 'cause I'm way be - yond you to - day.

To -

day I did-n't ev - en look to find

some-thing to put me in that peace _____ of mind. _____

You can't touch me 'cause I'm way _____ be-yond _____ you ___ to-day. _____

BOMFALLERALLA

Words and Music by HERBERT MUNKHAMMAR
and MAGNUS CARL ERIK LIDEHALL

Old-school Hip-Hop

B-b-b-bom - fal-le-ral-la, fal-le-ral-la, fal-le-ral-la
A - fa-fa-fa-si___ och Fil-

Bom - fal-le-ral-la, fal-le-ral-la, fal-le-ral-la.
thy.

Rap 1: (See additional lyrics)
Rap 2: (See additional lyrics)

R.H. tacet 1st time

* Recorded a half step lower

Copyright © 2004 UNIVERSAL MUSIC PUBLISHING AB, LIGHTS OUT PUBLISHING and SCANDINAVIAN SONGS AB
All Rights for UNIVERSAL MUSIC PUBLISHING AB in the U.S. and Canada Controlled and Administered by UNIVERSAL - POLYGRAM INTERNATIONAL PUBLISHING, INC.
All Rights for LIGHTS OUT PUBLISHING Administered by BMG RIGHTS MANAGEMENT (US) LLC
All Rights Reserved   Used by Permission

72

Ex - plo - der - ar som. **Rap 3:** *(See additional lyrics)*

Bom!

Nej flash. **Rap 4:** *(See additional lyrics)*

R.H. tacet 2nd time

bin, eld. Torrt krut och ben-sin. Shu-shu-ba shu-ba shu-ba snus, porr and bränn-vin.

Ritch ratch fil-i-bom-bom-bom. Ex-plo-der-ar som. Stu-

Ex - plo - der - ar som.

Additional Lyrics:

Rap 1:
Jag störtar ner för gatan på en Pamplona-tjur
På väg mot en Pandora-brud med ett klitta som en anabolakuk
Och svänger den röda skynket som fladdrar i vinden
Och flaggan som vajar och kladdande fradga på kinden, shhh
Jag är metallisk rakblad, smaka min tunga
Som jag kommer att hugga rakt från munnen som rabieshundar
Lätt garderad med ett artilleri
Som inte tar, tänker eller nånsin tatt ditt parti
Af-af-asi håller väckningsmässa
I en skoldress så ring och kör din text
Och hör mig gäspa som en flodhäst
Och när ni springer på glödheta kändisgalor
Känner jag hur det vänder i magen
På grund utav av era könslekar
Står du i min väg så betala vänligen trängselavgift
Oavsett om du är moderat eller vänsterpartist
För vi lever i en visslande tid som swishar förbi
Där jag gror i mitten och allt annat vissnar bredvid

Rap 3:
Du får på käften när vi tagit ett tugg
Och ställer upp dig mot mig med lika begåvade lyrik som en harlequin bok
Om jag nånsin faller i avgrunden ja då åker jag på värdekortet
Hela jävla vägen fram till pärleporten
Där st. per står och väntar med handen på gallret
Och en iskall stor stark och en varm hamburgertallrik
Och ni kan fortsätta stirra i porrblaskor
medan jag skingrar folkmassor som en brinnande Rolf Lassgård

Rap 2:
Jag blottar min bringa, måtte du hinna stånga mig
Så kom igen gör något motstånd innan du ångrar dig
Biter av stora kroppspulsådern
Som transporterar syre åt hela jävla världens dokusåper
Det är trist att jobba så jag sitter och joddlar
Och groggar vodka med diskmedel och fiskleverolja
Rätt vad det är så går ridån i botten, å nej
Där står jag och spakar testosteronet ur kroppen på dig
Befinner mig sen hos din bootylicius storasyster
Som ligger och sover på soffan med håret i toffsar
Skulle väl åka dit som en inbrottstjuv bara vips dyker upp
Som en tillbakaspolad simhopps brud
Tänjer på gränsen när ni främmande människor
Fryser för en kropp dom gått genom dom fem elementen
Men jag är väl förberedd för det som komma skall
Så jag laddar upp och slår tillbaka med ett bombanfall

Rap 4:
Jag är auktoritär som skyddsvästar och polisbrickor
Mens du är nyttig som ryggsäckar med mobilfickor
Herbert kan tricksa och fixa
Herbert kan micra en pizza
Herbert kan klippa och klistra och sitta och kissa
Jag tar mig fram lätt och smidigt i ett land
Jag skiter i den och bråkar med allting
Och låter som Styles P
Men jag slår mig fast vid och låter det aldrig
Gå så långt att jag talar ut i nån veckotidning
När min skit lackar ut är det ni som backar
Och åker likbil, snabbt akut i en kritvit svartkultur
Haha, sanningen svider jag vet
Men alla reppar ett skitet land på en liten planet

WITHOUT WORDS

Words and Music by RAY CHARLES
and JACK LaMONTAGNE

Moderate Folk beat

Step out - side the scene, they don't know you like I do.

Copyright © 2008 BMG Monarch and Sweet Mary Music
All Rights Administered by BMG Rights Management (US) LLC
All Rights Reserved   Used by Permission

They don't know you like I do.

Not all of life is cruel.

Not all of life is so un-true. Not all of life is so un-true.

I can hear the morning birds so light upon the branches. And each in turn, they sing of all God's praises. Yes, without words.

Without words.

Don't turn it all inside.

D7(sus2)   **Gmaj7**

I don't like to see you cry. _____ I don't

                      D   **Dmaj7**

like to see you cry. _____

Em   **A**

Whis - pered _____ kiss - es _____ in your _____ ears. _____

Em   **A**

A touch so soft and warm _____ as dew fall dis - ap - pears. _____

Con-fes-sions all of love for you. Yes, without words.

Stare in-to the flame 'til you see be-yond the light. All the while, truth was mine.

It's with my-self I fight. Sin you've car-ried like a corpse a-cross your back these days.

Let it fall away. Let it fall away.

Let it fall away.

D.S. al Coda

CODA

Without words.

NOT ABOUT ANGELS

Words and Music by
JASMINE VAN DEN BOGAERDE

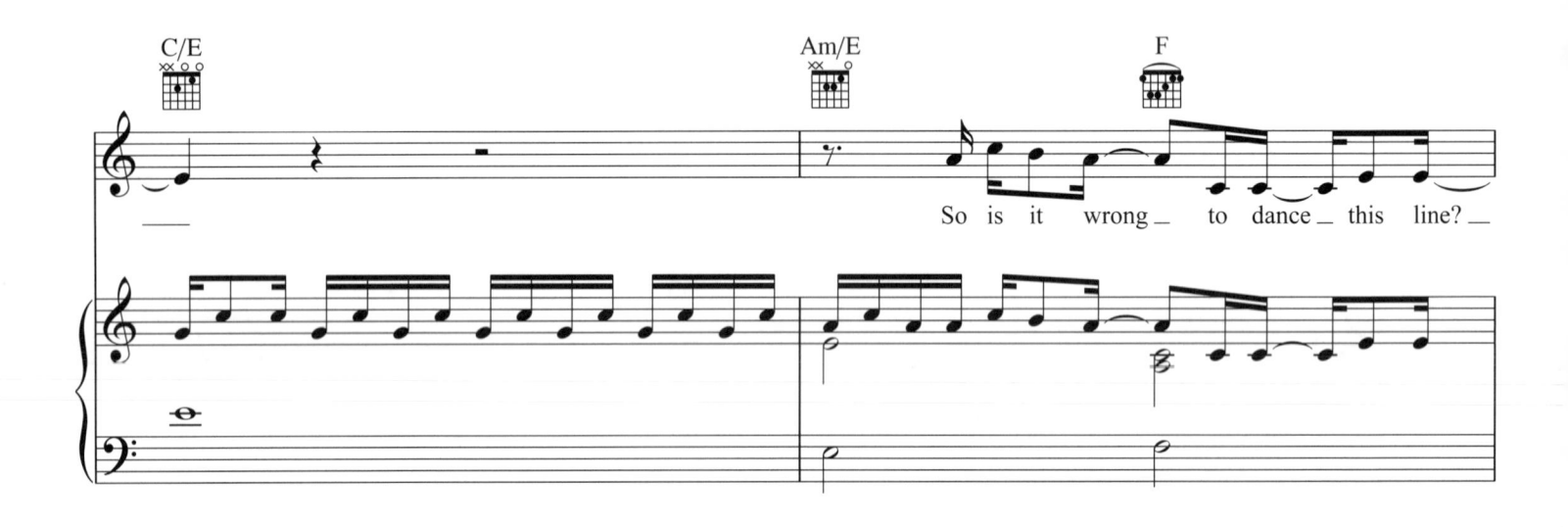

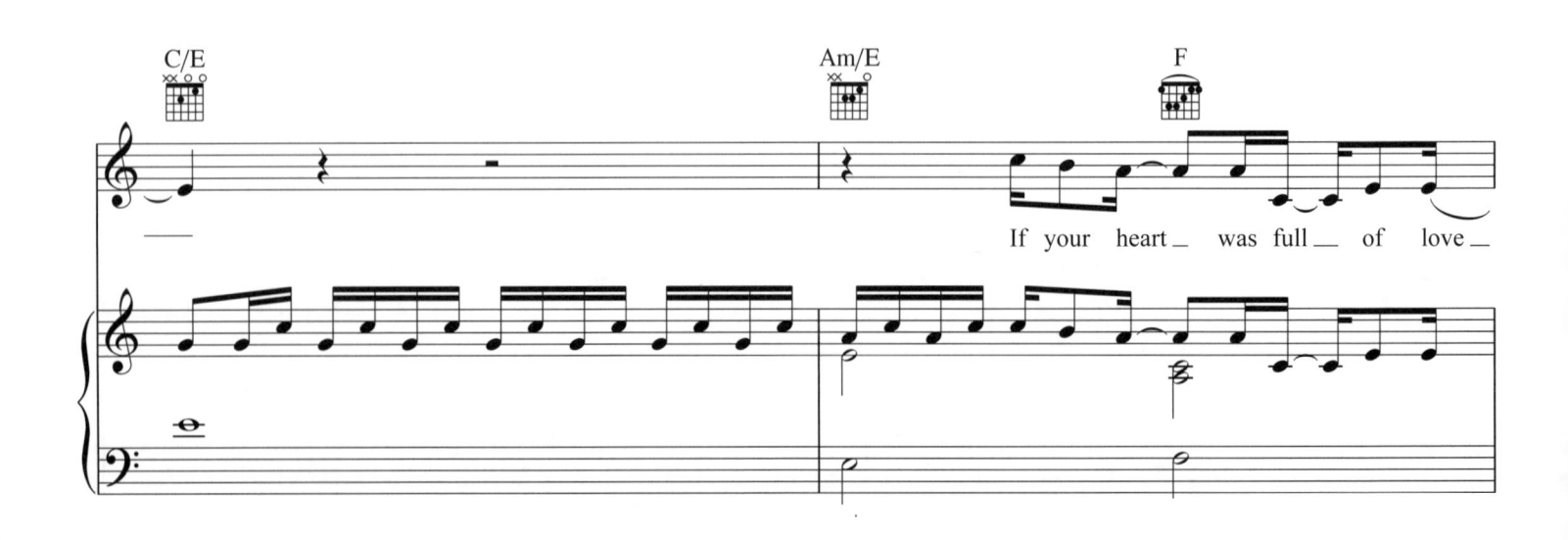

Moderately, with feeling

We know full well there's just time.

So is it wrong to dance this line?

If your heart was full of love

© 2014 GOOD SOLDIER SONGS LIMITED and T C F MUSIC PUBLISHING, INC.
All Rights for GOOD SOLDIER SONGS LIMITED in the U.S. and Canada Administered by WB MUSIC CORP.
All Rights Reserved   Used by Permission

could you give _____ it up?

'Cause what a-bout, what a-bout an - gels? _____

They will come, they will go and make us

spe - cial, oh. _____

Am F Em
Don't give me up.
Am F
Don't give me up.
C G/B Am F
How un - fair, it's just our luck.
C G/B Am F
Found some - thing real that's out of touch.

But if you'd searched the whole wide world, oh, would you dare to let it go?

'Cause what about, what about an - gels?

They will come, they will go and make us

F C Em
spe - cial, oh.
Am F Em
Don't give me up.
Am F
Don't give me up.
G F G
'Cause what a - bout, what a - bout an - gels?

They will come, they will go and make us spe - cial.

It's not a - bout, not a - bout an - gels, an - gels.

NO ONE EVER LOVED

Words and Music by LYKKE LI
and BJORN YTTLING

Moderate Ballad

No one ever loved, no one ever lost as hard as I. No one ever came, no one ever saw the crys-tal-line

Copyright © 2014 EMI April Music Inc.
All Rights Administered by Sony/ATV Music Publishing LLC, 424 Church Street, Suite 1200, Nashville, TN 37219
International Copyright Secured   All Rights Reserved

C Em G
in his eyes. Star - ry sky,
Am F C Em
par - a - dise in his eyes.
G Am F Am
In his arms, don't leave me now. Crys - tal - line,
G F
don't leave me now. You're the dia -

-mond in the gut-ter, you're the hole ___ in-side my heart. ___

You're the one ___ I will re-mem-ber ev-'ry night. ___

To Coda ⊕

be-fore ___ the dawn ___ meets the night. ___

Heav-en must have known, heav-en must have

Am F C Em G
laid star-dust in your eyes. Shine the light across the hurt
Am F C Em
into my eyes. See it now,
G Am F Am
pur - ple shrine was nev - er mine. An - gel line,
G F
you fell right down.
D.S. al Coda
You're the dia -

CODA

meets the light. And it kills me ev-e-ry time, ev-'ry star will fall right down.

Yeah, it kills me ev-e-ry time, ev-'ry star will fall right down.

G
C
Em
You're the dia - mond in the gut -
Am
C
Em
G
- ter, you're the hole in - side my heart. You're the one
C
Em
Am
F
Em
I will re - mem - ber ev - 'ry night. be - fore the dawn.
G7
C
Em
Am
You're the dia - mond in the gut - ter, you're the hole

C Em G C Em
inside my heart. You're the one I will remem-
Am F Em Dm
ber ev'ry night. before the dawn, ev-'ry
Em Dm Em
night 'fore the dawn, ev-'ry night 'fore the dawn
Dm Am Asus(add2) Am
meets the light.
rit.

WAIT

Words and Music by ANTHONY GONZALEZ,
YANN GONZALEZ and JUSTIN MELDAL-JOHNSEN

Moderately, dreamlike

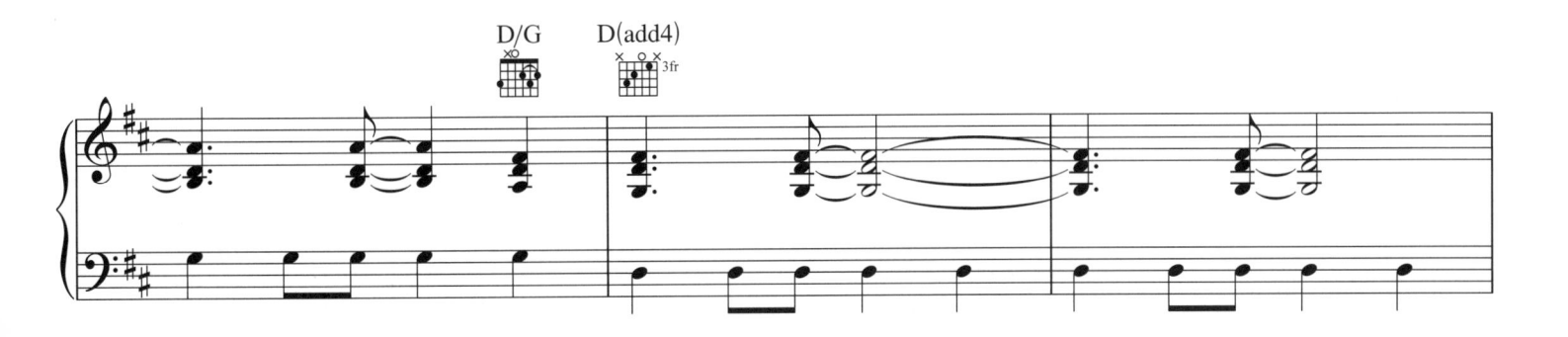

Send your dreams where no-bod-y
There's no end. There is no good-

D(add4)
3fr
hides.
bye.
Bm
G
Give
Dis -
your
ap -
tears
pear
to the
with the
tide.
night.
D(add4)
3fr
Bm

No time.

No time.

CODA
D/C♯
Bm
G
D
D/C♯
Play 3 times
No time.
Bm
G
D
D/C♯
Play 6 times
(Lead vocal ad lib.)
Bm
G
D

BEST SHOT

Words and Music by JASMINE VAN DEN BOGAERDE
and DAN WILSON

Light Acoustic Rock

When you're on your own__ and you feel__ lost.__ When your heart's a mess__ though you've giv-en__ your__ best. I'll be here giving it my best shot, baby, your love's got all that I need.

Here, crying from the rooftops, nothing can stop us if we believe.

Here, giving it my best shot, baby, I find that we can be free when you're here, here with me.

When your sky is dark and the earth is shak-ing your bed. Your hope is at its end, you just need one friend. I'll be

CODA

Mmm. When you can't find your way and all

D.S. al Coda

a - round you wa - ter's deep and grey. The stars fall from _a - bove_ and _you're bare - ly hold - ing on, my love, on my love._ Giv - ing it my best shot, ba - by, your love's got all that I need.

| Am | B♭ | F |

Here, cry-ing from the roof-tops, noth-ing can stop us if we be-lieve.

| C | B♭ | F |

Here, giv-ing it my best shot, ba-by, I find

| C | Dm | B♭ |

that we can be free when you're here,

| F |

here with me.